WORLD'S SCARIEST CREATURES

BY JOHN LESLEY

FIERCE REPTILES

Gareth Stevens PUBLISHING

**Please visit our website,
www.garethstevens.com.
For a free color catalog of all
our high-quality books, call
toll free 1-800-542-2595 or
fax 1-877-542-2596.**

Cataloging-in-Publication Data
Names: Lesley, John.
Title: Fierce reptiles / John Lesley.
Description: Buffalo, NY : Gareth Stevens Publishing, 2026. |
Series: World's scariest creatures | Includes glossary and index.
Identifiers: ISBN 9781482474084 (pbk.) | ISBN 9781482474091
(library bound) | ISBN 9781482474107 (ebook)
Subjects: LCSH: Reptiles--Juvenile literature.
Classification: LCC QL644.2 L475 2026 | DDC 597.9--dc23

Published in 2026 by
Gareth Stevens Publishing
2544 Clinton St.
Buffalo, NY 14224

First published 2025 by Redback Publishing

Author: John Lesley
Editor: Simone Saba
Designer: Redback Publishing
Original illustrations © Redback Publishing 2025
Originated by Redback Publishing

Acknowledgements
Abbreviations: l—left, r—right, b—bottom,
t—top, c—centre, m—middle

We would like to thank the following for permission to reproduce photographs (images © Shutterstock unless otherwise stated)

Printed in the United States of America

CPSIA compliance information: Batch #CSGS26
For further information contact Gareth Stevens at 1-800-542-2595.

Find us on

CONTENTS

Komodo Dragon 4

Gila Monster 6

Frill-necked Lizard 8

Crocodile 10

Turtles and Tortoises 12

Thorny Devil 14

Chameleon 16

Snakes 18

How Are Reptiles Special? 20

More Reptiles 22

World's Scariest Reptiles 24

Are They Dinosaurs? 26

Reptiles as Pets 28

Glossary (Reptile Word List) 31

Index 32

KOMODO DRAGON

Varanus Komodoensis

Komodo dragons, also known Komodo monitors, are large, fearsome reptiles that are native to the Indonesian islands of Komodo, Rinca, and Flores. They are the largest species of lizard in the world and are known for their massive size and powerful jaws.

LIFE CYCLE

After a gestation period of about 8 months, female Komodo dragons will lay a clutch of over 20 eggs, which will hatch after about 9 months. Baby Komodo dragons are born fully formed and are able to hunt for food on their own almost immediately. Komodo dragons live for about 30 years in the wild.

HABITAT

The Komodo dragon now only lives in the wild in the Indonesian Komodo National Park and on the island of Flores. They prefer habitats that are close to water, such as savannas, forests, and grasslands, and they are most active during the day.

FOOD

Komodo dragons are carnivores, which means that they eat meat. They feed mainly on deer, pigs, and goats, but they are also known to eat smaller mammals, birds, and other reptiles.

FACT

Komodo dragons are the largest species of lizard in the world.

FACT FILE

Length: up to 9.8 feet (3 m)
Color: sandy or gray with camouflaging dark lines and spots
Venomous: yes
Habitat: savannas, forests, and grasslands
Lifespan: more than 30 years
Scientific name: *Varanus Komodoensis*

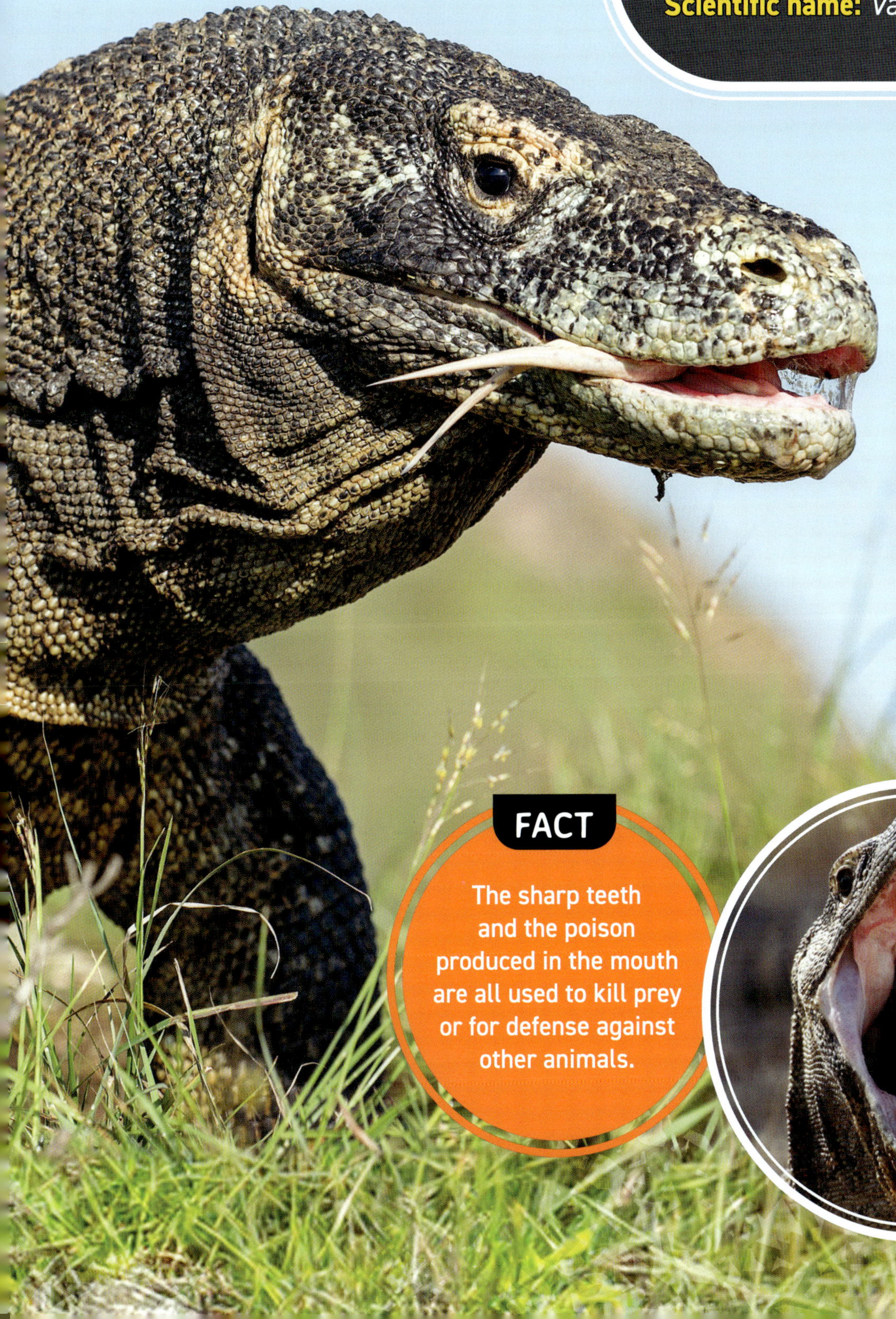

The forked tongue flicks constantly in and out to get information from scent particles in the air.

FACT

The sharp teeth and the poison produced in the mouth are all used to kill prey or for defense against other animals.

GILA MONSTER

Heloderma suspectum

The Gila monster is one of only a few venomous lizards in the world. It has a distinctive appearance. They have a bead-like skin texture, which is composed of osteoderms (bony deposits) covered with scales.

LIFE CYCLE

Females lay their eggs in burrows or under rocks. The eggs hatch after about four months, and the young are independent from birth.

HABITAT

Gila monsters are native to the southwestern United States and northwestern Mexico. They inhabit arid and semiarid regions, including deserts, scrublands, and rocky foothills.

FOOD

Gila monsters are carnivorous and have a diet that includes small mammals, birds, eggs, lizards, and insects. They have a slow metabolism and can survive on a few large meals a year, storing fat in their tails.

VENOM AND BITING

Gila monsters have venom glands located in their lower jaws. Their venom is delivered through grooves in their teeth as they chew on their prey. The venom is used mainly for defense rather than hunting.

FACT

Gila monsters can deliver a painful and venomous bite.

FACT

Gila monsters are excellent climbers.

FACT FILE

Length: 20 to 24 inches (50 to 61 cm)
Color: black with patterns of pink, orange, or yellow
Venomous: yes
Habitat: arid and semiarid regions
Lifespan: 20-30 years
Scientific name: *Heloderma suspectum*

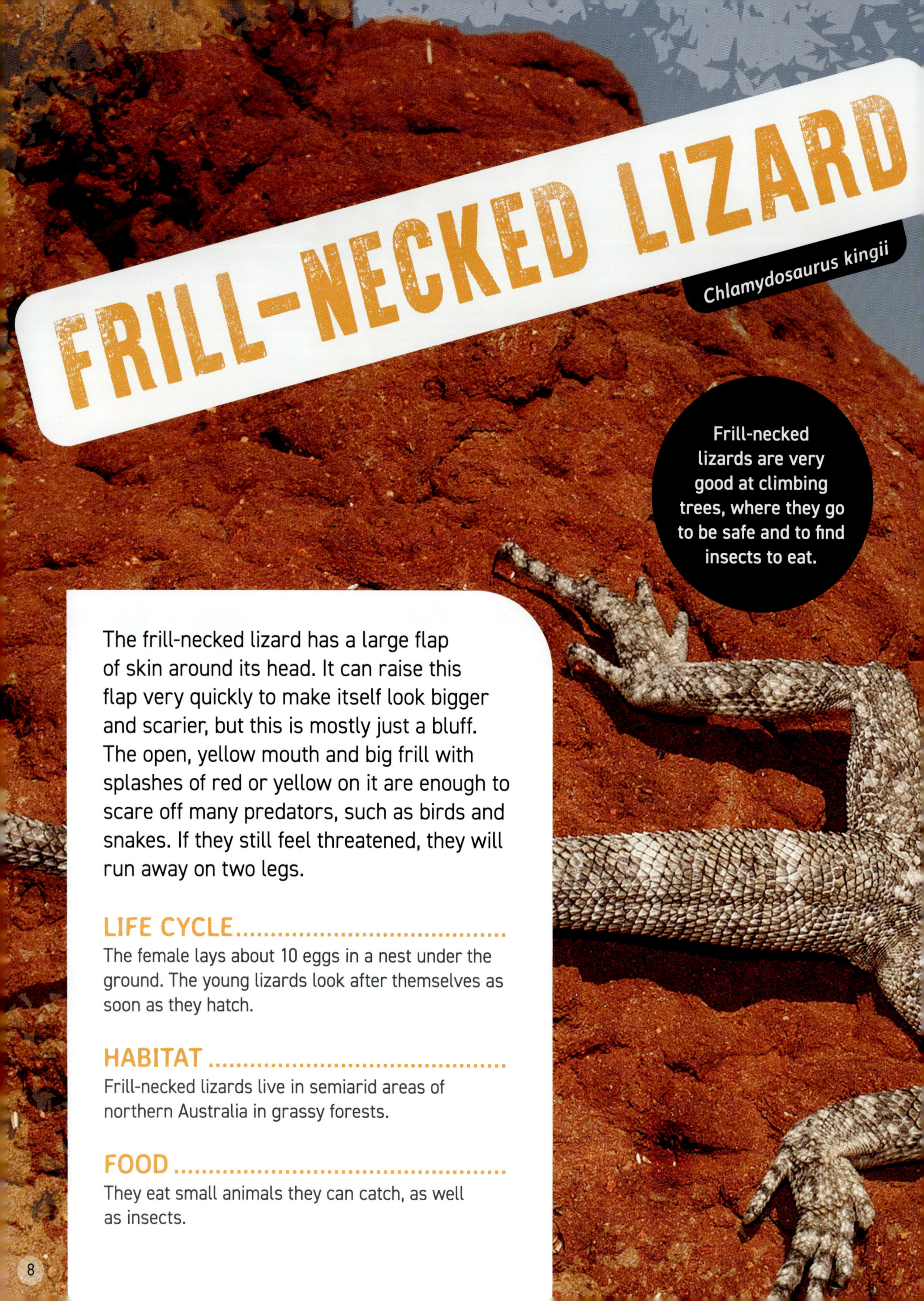

FRILL-NECKED LIZARD

Chlamydosaurus kingii

Frill-necked lizards are very good at climbing trees, where they go to be safe and to find insects to eat.

The frill-necked lizard has a large flap of skin around its head. It can raise this flap very quickly to make itself look bigger and scarier, but this is mostly just a bluff. The open, yellow mouth and big frill with splashes of red or yellow on it are enough to scare off many predators, such as birds and snakes. If they still feel threatened, they will run away on two legs.

LIFE CYCLE

The female lays about 10 eggs in a nest under the ground. The young lizards look after themselves as soon as they hatch.

HABITAT

Frill-necked lizards live in semiarid areas of northern Australia in grassy forests.

FOOD

They eat small animals they can catch, as well as insects.

FACT

Males fight each other by biting and showing off their frills.

FACT FILE

Length: up to 3.3 feet (1 m)
Color: mottled brown, gray, and sandy scales
Venomous: no
Habitat: semiarid areas of Australia with open forests
Lifespan: about 10 years in the wild
Scientific name: *Chlamydosaurus kingii*

CONSERVATION

Because it lives in remote areas, the frill-necked lizard is not under threat of extinction at present.

VENOM AND BITING

Frill-necked lizards do not have venom, but they will bite you if you threaten them. They have very sharp teeth.

CROCODILE

Crocodylus

There are three primary species of crocodiles: saltwater crocodiles, American crocodiles, and Nile crocodiles. There are several other species and subspecies of crocodiles, some of which are less well-known.

LIFE CYCLE

The female crocodile lays eggs in a nest beside the water. She usually guards the nest until the babies hatch.

HABITAT

Crocodiles are primarily aquatic reptiles and are well-adapted to both freshwater and saltwater environments. Crocodiles are cold-blooded reptiles that rely on external sources of heat to regulate their body temperature. They bask in the sun to warm up and retreat to water or shade to cool down.

FACT

Cassius is a male saltwater croc living in captivity on Green Island in the Great Barrier Reef Australia.

He is over 120 years old!

In some parts of the world, there are as many crocs as humans!

FACT FILE

Length: up to 19.7 feet (6 m)
Color: dark, mottled browns and grays
Venomous: no
Habitat: fresh and salty water, and its nearby land
Lifespan: up to 70 years
Scientific name:
Crocodylus porosus (saltwater crocodile)
Crocodylus niloticus (Nile crocodile)
Crocodylus acutus (American crocodile)

FACT

AS OLD AS DINOSAURS

Saltwater crocodiles are some of the oldest kinds of creatures walking the planet.

FOOD

Crocodiles are carnivores, which means they eat meat. They hunt animals by lying still under the water and waiting for prey to come to them. They will grab prey in the water, from the edge of a river or lake, or off a beach.

VENOM AND BITING

Crocodiles do not have venom, but their bite can be lethal. To kill their prey, they bite them and then may drag them under the water to drown.

TURTLES AND TORTOISES

Turtles and tortoises are reptiles. Their shell is a part of their spine, and it is an adaptation to help protect them from predators.

Sea turtles live in water most of the time, and they have evolved to have flippers and webbed feet. These turtles need to come onto land to lay their eggs.

Freshwater turtles live on land and in creeks and lakes in a variety of habitats, including forests, grasslands, and deserts.

FLATBACK SEA TURTLE
LEATHERBACK SEA TURTLE
HAWKSBILL SEA TURTLE

THORNY DEVIL

Moloch horridus

The thorny devil lizard is completely covered in large thorn-like spikes. These spikes have two important purposes. They protect the lizard from attack, but they also channel drops of dew down to the mouth. This is often the only water source these lizards have in their desert environment.

LIFE CYCLE

The female lays about 10 eggs in a burrow. They hatch after about three months.

HABITAT

Thorny devils live in desert habitats, where their sandy colors help to camouflage them from predators.

FOOD

Thorny devils eat ants. This single food source makes thorny devils vulnerable to any change in their habitat that would affect the ant population.

CONSERVATION

Thorny devils are not presently under any threat of extinction, largely due to living in isolated, desert regions.

FACT

A thorny devil has a lump that looks like a second head on the back of its neck. This is probably used to confuse predators.

FACT

They can eat 3,000 ants in one meal.

Thorny devils are small, only about 8 inches (20 cm) long.

FACT FILE

Length: about 8 inches (20 cm)
Color: yellow, brown, and orange
Habitat: deserts
Lifespan: over 10 years
Scientific name: *Moloch horridus*

CHAMELEON

Chamaeleonidae

Chameleons are famous for their strange look, the way they move, and for their ability to change color. This ability is used for communication, temperature regulation, and camouflage. They change color through the expansion and contraction of specialized cells called chromatophores.

LIFE CYCLE

Most chameleons are oviparous, laying eggs in the soil. The number of eggs and the incubation period vary by species. Some chameleons are ovoviviparous, giving birth to live young.

HABITAT

They are primarily found in Africa and Madagascar, but some species are also found in southern Europe, the Middle East, and parts of Asia and India. They inhabit a variety of environments, including rainforests, savannas, and sometimes deserts.

FACT

The chameleon can rotate and focus its eyes separately to look at two different objects at the same time!

FACT FILE

Length: up to 27 inches (68 cm)
Color: adaptive multicolor
Venomous: no
Habitat: rainforests and savannas
Lifespan: around 6 years
Scientific name: *Chamaeleonidae*

They have a long, sticky tongue that can be rapidly extended to catch prey.

SNAKES

Snakes are reptiles that have lost their legs. This adaptation enables them to hide in narrow areas between rocks. Not having legs does not stop snakes from climbing trees or getting up into the roofs of houses.

LIFE CYCLE

Snakes lay soft eggs. After hatching, the young snakes are usually able to look after themselves right away. Some snakes can live for 20 years.

HABITAT

Snakes live in most habitats, including rainforests, grasslands, in fresh water and the ocean, on farmland, and in deserts. Some snakes are very happy living near houses and towns.

FOOD

Snakes are carnivores. They hunt their prey and swallow it whole. Some snakes inject venom into their prey before eating it. Pythons do not have venom, but they crush their prey to kill it before swallowing it.

CONSERVATION

Some types of snakes are under threat of extinction, while others are thriving.

VENOM AND BITING

Some snakes have venom, and they bite. Their venom can be deadly to humans.

COPPERHEAD
SEA SNAKE
GREEN TREE PYTHON
CHILDREN'S PYTHON
DEATH ADDER
BLIND SNAKE
TAIPAN
TIGER SNAKE
DIAMOND PYTHON
RED-BELLIED BLACK SNAKE

HOW ARE REPTILES SPECIAL?

Reptiles mostly lay eggs, although some produce live young that are ready to run off and look after themselves soon after birth.

Some reptiles are highly intelligent and are even able to count.

Reptile eggs usually have soft shells, making them less likely to crack when they are buried in underground nests.

Snakes are reptiles that don't have legs.

They are cold-blooded, which means they need the heat from the sun or their surroundings to become warm enough to move around.

Reptiles have scales that give them a strong outer covering.

The scaly skin is shed in sheets so that the reptile can grow bigger.

Reptiles mostly have claws and sharp teeth.

MORE REPTILES

CENTRAL NETTED DRAGON
MARY RIVER TURTLE
EASTERN LONG-NECKED TURTLE
GREEN TURTLE
BEARDED DRAGON
LACE MONITOR

WORLD'S SCARIEST REPTILES

PERENTIE - AUSTRALIA

RED-BELLIED BLACK SNAKE - AUSTRALIA

RATTLESNAKE - NORTH AND SOUTH AMERICA

KOMODO DRAGON - INDONESIA

KING COBRA - ASIA

GHARIAL - INDIA

ANACONDA - SOUTH AMERICA

The scariest reptile that ever lived was probably the *T. rex*.

Fortunately, we are separated from it by many millions of years!

SALTWATER CROCODILE - AUSTRALIA

ALLIGATOR SNAPPING TURTLE - USA

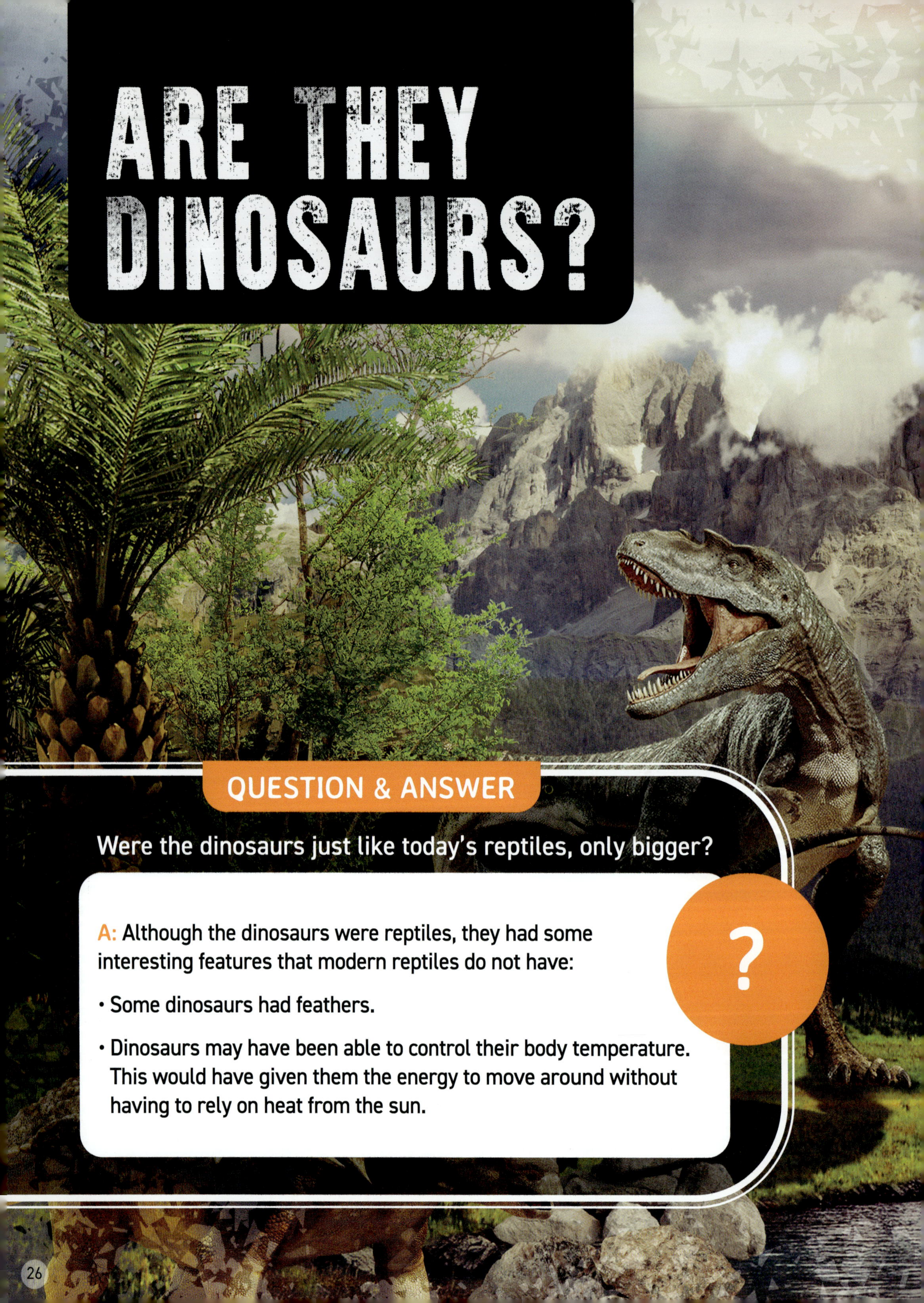

ARE THEY DINOSAURS?

QUESTION & ANSWER

Were the dinosaurs just like today's reptiles, only bigger?

A: Although the dinosaurs were reptiles, they had some interesting features that modern reptiles do not have:

- Some dinosaurs had feathers.
- Dinosaurs may have been able to control their body temperature. This would have given them the energy to move around without having to rely on heat from the sun.

QUESTION & ANSWER

?

Are all reptiles descended from dinosaurs?

A: No! Dinosaurs existed at the same time as the ancestors of crocodiles, snakes, and lizards. They all lived on Earth at the same time, millions of years ago, but each evolved into different types of animals that are alive today. The dinosaurs seem to have been the ancestors of modern birds, not of lizards, snakes, or crocodiles.

?

Were the dinosaurs reptiles?

A: Yes! Dinosaurs were reptiles.

REPTILES AS PETS

Reptiles can make fascinating and rewarding pets for enthusiasts willing to invest time and effort in their care. Proper research into the species' needs and requirements, along with commitment to providing a suitable environment, diet, and veterinary care, are crucial to ensuring the welfare and longevity of a pet reptile.

LACE MONITOR

THORNY DEVIL

DESERT PLANT

ROUGH-SCALED SNAKE

GLOSSARY

Reptile Word List

ancestors living things in the past from which modern life has come

bluff a show or false claim of something

burrow hole in the ground that is an animal's home

camouflage shapes or colors that help an animal hide in their habitat

carnivore animal that eats meat

dew water droplets that form out of the air

evolve change over time

extinction when all animals of one type are dead

forked split into two parts

isolated not being near other things

omnivore animal that eats both meat and plants

semiarid area with low rainfall

stable steady and not changing

thriving growing well and reproducing

venom poison produced by an animal to kill prey or defend itself

webbed feet having skin between the toes

FRESHWATER CROCODILE FOOT

INDEX

biting 6, 9, 11, 18

camouflage 14, 16, 31

claws 21

cold-blooded 10, 21, 26

dinosaurs 11, 25-27

eggs 4, 6, 8, 10, 12, 14, 16, 18, 20

extinction 9, 14, 18, 31

scales 6, 9, 21

venom 5-7, 9, 11, 17, 18, 31